The King is Coming

Easter

W. Dean Witten

1

Dedicated to the Glory of God

In gratitude

For God's Salvation Story

ATTRIBUTIONS

Complimentary editing services provided by Wendell Witten and Lisa Witten Williams.

ISBN-13:978-1985817593

ISBN-10:1985817594

Printed by CreateSpace, an Amazon.com Company
Available from Amazon.com, CreateSpace.com, and other retail outlets.
Available on Kindle and other retail outlets

ABOUT THE AUTHOR

W. Dean Witten is a 1960 graduate of Florida Southern College with a Bachelor of Arts degree and a 1963 graduate of the Methodist Theological School in Ohio with a Master of Divinity degree. Florida Southern also honored him with a Doctor of Divinity degree.

He has served as pastor of seven United Methodist churches. In addition, he served as superintendent of the Sarasota and Orlando districts of the Florida Conference UMC, 1992 to 2002. After 41 years of service he retired in June 2002.

Books Written by W. Dean Witten

Does God Really Care About Me?
Connecting the Dots

God's Story: Advent & Christmas

God's Story: Good Friday & Easter

Living Through the Storms: Job's Story

Questions for God: Seeking Clarity

Jesus' Questions for Present Day
Christians

Praying Like Jesus through the Storms of Life

Living in an Unsafe World: Reflections on
Psalm 23

The Beatitudes of Jesus

The King is Coming: Advent & Christmas

The King is Coming: Epiphany

The King is Coming: Lent

These books are available at
Amazon.com, CreateSpace.com, and
other retail outlets.

Table of Contents

Preface

The King is Coming! When? We just don't know the timeline but we do know the storyline. The first three volumes of this series trace it through Advent, Christmas, Epiphany, and Lent. The scriptures for God's story are found in the both the Old Testament and the New.

This fourth volume of the King is Coming series focuses for the most part on gospel readings for Easter, which recount major events from the resurrection story.

This book of devotions is designed for reliving God's Story. While walking in the footsteps of the first Christians through the gospel witness, present day Christians will reflect and meditate on gospel selections which track the journey of Christ the King from the tomb to the Ascension.

Remember that God's Story did not happen in a vacuum. The reality is that it played out in real time, in the land of Palestine, and is preserved in the Bible. We are blessed to hear it anew and relive it in the Twenty First Century.

Easter Sunday
Matthew 28:1-9

"After the sabbath, as the first day of the week was dawning, Mary Magdalene and the other Mary went to see the tomb. And suddenly there was a great earthquake; for an angel of the Lord, descending from heaven, came and rolled back the stone and sat on it. His appearance was like lightning, and his clothing white as snow. For fear of him the guards shook and became like dead men. But the angel said to the women, 'Do not be afraid; I know that you are looking for Jesus who was crucified. He is not here; for he has been raised, as he said. Come, see the place where he lay. Then go quickly and tell his disciples, He has been raised from the dead, and indeed he is going ahead of you to Galilee; there you will see him. This is my message for you.' So they left the tomb quickly with fear and great joy, and ran to tell his disciples. Suddenly Jesus met them and said, 'Greetings!' And they came to him, took hold of his feet, and worshiped him."

"Surprised!"

The two women were not Easter people when they arrived at the tomb. Instead, they were realists. They knew that Jesus was dead and dead meant finished. Neither Mary expected ever again to see him alive. And they were stunned by the young man in a white robe sitting on the stone door to the tomb who said to them, "I know you are looking for Jesus, who was crucified. He is not here; for he has been raised from the dead."

The angel's message was confusing. Within three days the tomb was empty. His body was gone. The women inspected the holy sepulcher and could not find it. To this day, the tomb is still empty. Moreover, no one expects to find Jesus' body or remains anywhere on the face of the earth.

The women turned to leave. They were afraid, yet filled with joy. Then Jesus met them.

"Greetings," he said. "And they came to him, took hold of his feet and worshiped him."

That is the good news. "He has been raised from the dead." The resurrection of Jesus Christ has demolished the boundar es of human existence and given us living hope in the face of death. "Because I live," to use his words from the gospel, "you shall live also." This means that even in the face of death, we do in fact have a future.

The message of Easter is still the same. "He is not here. He has been raised from the dead." And this is good news in a world where life is fragile and our days are numbered. There's hope! "Because he lives I car face tomorrow."

Sing and/or Listen

"Because He Lives"
s://www.youtube.com/watch?v=spa7WkwjwG
w

Pray
Heavenly Father, I stand amazed in the presence
of the mystery of Christ's resurrection. Hard for
me to wrap my mind around it. Nevertheless, I
am grateful and celebrate it again this day.
Amen.

The Spiritual Discipline of Journaling

A way to concentrate on being in God's presence.

1. Read the selected scripture passage. Record your immediate thoughts.

2. Read the devotion/reflection for today. Record your thoughts and/or write your personal reflections.

3. Prayerfully listen for God's message to you. Record what you hear from the Lord.

4. Pray the prayer that is written and/or record and pray your own prayer.

5. Conclude with praise and worship. Use the suggested hymn from YouTube or choose another.

On the Road to Emmaus

Luke 24:13-35

"Now on that same day two of them were going to a village called Emmaus ... and talking with each other about all these things that had happened. ... Jesus himself came near and went with them, but their eyes were kept from recognizing him. ... Then he said to them, 'Oh, how foolish you are, and how slow of heart to believe all that the prophets have declared! Was it not necessary that the Messiah should suffer these things and then enter into his glory?' Then beginning with Moses and all the prophets, he interpreted to them the things about himself in all the scriptures. As they came near the village to which they were going ... they urged him strongly, saying, 'Stay with us, because it is almost evening and the day is now nearly over. ...' When he was at the table with them, he took bread, blessed and broke it, and gave it to them. Then their eyes were opened, and they recognized him. ... Then they told ... how he had been made known to them in the breaking of the bread."

"He took bread, blessed and broke it, and gave it to them"

Two disciples returning home from Jerusalem on Easter Sunday kindly invited a stranger to spend the evening with them. As they were eating super the stranger took the bread, blessed and broke it, and gave it to them. Jesus had also done that at the Last Supper on Maundy Thursday when he instituted the Sacrament of Holy Communion. Blessing, breaking and giving the

17

bread was a distinctively "Jesus thing" to do.
Then their eyes were opened and they recognized him "when he broke the bread."

At that very moment,
Their table became his Holy Table.
They communed with the living Christ.
They became Easter people.
It was a God-born, God-directed,
God-sustained experience.
Jesus transformed their table into his Holy
Table,
Rebirthed them as Easter people,
Formatted a redemption-wrapped
celebration.

Easter People still return to his Table,
Where Christ blesses and breaks the bread,
Where Christ engages us in Holy Conversation,
Where Christ hears confession and grants
forgiveness,
Where Holy Covenant is renewed and the
church is united.

The Holy Table is a surefire sign of Jesus with us.

Prayer

Lord, I/we rejoice that you are host of the Holy Table. Help me/us to recognize you in the breaking of the bread and the blessing of the cup. Amen.

Sing and/or Listen!

https://www.youtube.com/watch?v=s4l2yY2r9 5g

Fill my cup Lord, I lift it up, Lord!
Come and quench this thirsting of my soul;
Bread of heaven, Feed me till I want no more
Fill my cup, fill it up and make me whole!
-The United Methodist Hymnal # 641

The Spiritual Discipline of Journaling

A way to concentrate on being in God's presence.

1. Read the selected scripture passage. Record your immediate thoughts.

2. Read the devotion/reflection for today. Record your thoughts and/or write your personal reflections.

3. Prayerfully listen for God's message to you. Record what you hear from the Lord.

4. Pray the prayer that is written and/or record and pray your own prayer.

5. Conclude with praise and worship. Use the suggested hymn from YouTube or choose another.

Monday

In the Upper Room

This is God's Story

John 20:19-35

"When it was evening on that day, the first day of the week, and the doors of the house where the disciples had met were locked for fear of the Jews, Jesus came and stood among them and said, 'Peace be with you.' After he said this, he showed them his hands and his side. Then the disciples rejoiced when they saw the Lord."

"He stood among them"

Harry Houdini was a master at escape. Even though he lived in the first quarter of the 20th century, most have read about his fantastic, incredible feats. Chained and handcuffed, he was locked in trunks and dumped into rivers, but he always managed to escape before drowning. But when appendicitis struck him in 1926, Harry Houdini, who had perfected the art of escape, could not free himself from the chains of death.

Death is inescapable. Secular people know that is true. Confirmation is everywhere. One may delay it but one cannot finally escape from it. Yet, Christ did. He rose from the dead. Moreover, "Jesus came and stood among them."

The French thinker, Auguste Comte, once told Thomas Carlyle that he was going to start a new religion which would replace Christianity. "Very good," replied Carlyle. "All you have to do is to be crucified, rise again the third day, and get the world to believe you are still alive. Then your new religion will have a chance."

Jesus Christ did that. He came to the Upper Room on the evening of Easter Day and stood among some disciples. Each saw him with his own eyes, talked with him, and heard him say, "peace be with you."

What a relief! "They were glad when they saw the Lord." Of course, they were glad! How could it be otherwise, considering that he died and was buried on the previous Friday? Jesus Christ is alive, now and forevermore!

Sing and or Listen

https://www.youtube.com/watch?v=lgy7g6BCNOO

He touched me, Oh He touched me,
"And oh the joy that floods my soul!
Something happened and now I know,
He touched me and made me whole."

Pray

Dear Lord, King Jesus, I too rejoice that you are alive, now and forevermore. I look for your return. Amen.

The Spiritual Discipline of Journaling

A way to concentrate on being in God's presence.

1. Read the selected scripture passage. Record your immediate thoughts.

2. Read the devotion/reflection for today. Record your thoughts and/or write your personal reflections.

3. Prayerfully listen for God's message to you. Record what you hear from the Lord.

4. Pray the prayer that is written and/or record and pray your own prayer.

5. Conclude with praise and worship. Use the suggested hymn from YouTube or choose another.

Tuesday

Easter People

Matthew 28:1-10

"But the angel said to the women, 'Do not be afraid; I know that you are looking for Jesus who was crucified. He is not here; for he has been raised, as he said. Come, see the place where he lay. Then go quickly and tell his disciples, 'He has been raised from the dead, and indeed he is going ahead of you to Galilee; there you will see him. This is my message for you.' So they left the tomb quickly with fear and great joy, and ran to tell his disciples. Suddenly Jesus met them and said, 'Greetings!' And they came to him, took hold of his feet, and worshipped him. Then Jesus said to them, 'Do not be afraid; go and tell my brothers to go to Galilee; there they will see me.'"

"We are Easter People"

They were not Easter people!
No one expected his Resurrection!
Not the two Marys at the tomb,
Not even Peter or the other disciples in hiding.
He was dead.
Get it?
Dead!
Dead!
Dead!

Not one disciple hiding behind the bushes,
Just waiting for Jesus to walk out of the tomb.
No one, absolutely no one, keeping Easter Vigil,
Because dead was dead.

God intervened with Sunday and the miracle of
resurrection.
Jesus appeared to the women.
They were shocked,
Yet filled with joy.
Speechless,
Yet filled with adoration and praise.

Today the relentless and persistent witness of
the church is clear,
"He has been raised."
Nevertheless,
Millions still do not believe in the resurrection
of Jesus,
But we do.
We are Easter people!

Praise God! We have hope because Jesus is
alive, now and forevermore!

Sing and/listen

"Easter People, Raise Your Voices"

https://www.youtube.com/watch?v=uA4kiv8IS
Kg

Easter people, raise your voices, sounds of
heaven in earth should ring.
Christ has brought us heaven's choices; heavenly music, let us ring.
Alleluia! Alleluia! Easter people let us sing.

Prayer

God, I am so grateful for the promise of Easter.
The good news fills me and the whole church
with hope and the joy of life. Thank you that
death was not the final word about Jesus. Nor is
it the final word about us. We praise you, O God,
for your Salvation Story which assures eternal
life! Amen.

The Spiritual Discipline of Journaling

A way to concentrate on being in God's presence.

1. Read the selected scripture passage. Record your immediate thoughts.

2. Read the devotion/reflection for today. Record your thoughts and/or write your personal reflections.

3. Prayerfully listen for God's message to you. Record what you hear from the Lord.

4. Pray the prayer that is written and/or record and pray your own prayer.

5. Conclude with praise and worship. Use the suggested hymn from YouTube or choose another.

Wednesday

"I know that my Redeemer lives . . ."
Job 19:25-26

John 11: 25

Jesus said to her, "I am the resurrection and the life. Those who believe in me, even though they die, will live."

"He Lives"

Job said, "I know that my Redeemer lives, and that at the last he will stand upon the earth; and after my skin has been thus destroyed, then in my flesh I shall see God, whom I shall see on my side, and my eyes shall behold, and not another."

How did Job know? How could he be so sure? How can anyone? Faith is the answer. Neither science nor logic is of any help. There is only faith, faith in the God of mercy and justice. It is as Mother Teresa of Calcutta said to her superiors, "I have three pennies and a dream from God to build an orphanage." Her superiors chided gently, "Mother Teresa, you cannot build an orphanage with three pennies. With three pennies, you can't do anything." Smiling, she responded, "I know, but with God and three pennies I can do anything!"

Job's faith was like that. He had an epiphany of his Redeemer! Consequently, his confidence was unsurpassed. He roared, "I know my redeemer lives . . . I shall see God . . . on my side . . ."

That's our faith as well. Joan and I sent our 2014 Easter greeting to family via email on Easter day. The greeting said:

Because

William Albert Witten & Alphoretta LeMaster

lived

And Because

Arthur Lester Duke & Alice Ellon Edmund lived

We have this Easter to Celebrate

And Because

Jesus lives

We have Easter forever!

That is the faith which encourages and sustains us as we contemplate the inevitable end of life. "Easter forever" has been and is an incredibly wonderful life sustaining conviction.

Prove it! We cannot. Nevertheless, we are convinced death is not the end. As Job said, "I know that my Redeemer lives." And Jesus the Christian Redeemer said in the gospel story, "I am the resurrection and the life. Those who believe in me, even though they die, will live, and everyone who lives and believes in me will never die."

That is indeed good news. God did step into human existence and reversed the ending of our life story through the life and resurrection of Jesus Christ. Thanks to him we have Easter forever. Amen!

"Come, Christians, Join to Sing"
Sing and/or Listen
https://www.youtube.com/watch?v=UEpjJMW0lZY

Pray

Christ the King! As you have given us eternal life through your resurrection, give me the desire to live to serve you and you alone. Give me strength in my weakness to live as a person whose King has triumphed over death and whose kingdom is eternal. Forgive me when I fall short of your glory. Amen.

The Spiritual Discipline of Journaling

A way to concentrate on being in God's presence.

1. Read the selected scripture passage. Record your immediate thoughts.

2. Read the devotion/reflection for today. Record your thoughts and/or write your personal reflections.

3. Prayerfully listen for God's message to you. Record what you hear from the Lord.

4. Pray the prayer that is written and/or record and pray your own prayer.

5. Conclude with praise and worship. Use the suggested hymn from YouTube or choose another.

Thursday

"The Inheritance"
1 Peter 1:3-9

"Inheritance" is Peter's word in the Epistle selection. Here is a modern word picture of what it means for us through the living Christ.

A legendary story made the made the email rounds regarding a fabulously wealthy man who loved his son. They began to build an art collection together. They spent every spare minute searching for works of art, including Picasso and Raphael. They built a rare and valuable collections.

When the Vietnam conflict broke out, the son went off to war. He wrote his dad every day. One day the letters stopped and his father received a telegram from the war department informing that his son had been killed while attempting to rescue another soldier. Father was heartbroken.

Six months later, a young soldier carrying a large package knocked at the father's door. He introduced himself as the soldier for whom the man's son had sacrificed his life. He explained that in gratitude he had painted a picture of his son and wanted to give it to his father because his son had often shared that he and his father loved art.

The father hung the portrait over his mantle. When visitors came to his home, he always drew attention to the portrait of his son before he showed them any of the other masterpieces.

Eventually, the father died and his entire collection was offered at an exclusive private auction. Collectors and art experts gathered for the chance of purchasing one of them.

To everyone's surprise, the first painting on the auction block was the soldier's modest rendering of his son. The auctioneer pounded his gavel and asked someone to start the bidding. The sophisticated crowd scoffed and demanded the Van Gogh's and the Rembrandts. The auctioneer persisted. "Who will start the bidding? $200? $100?" The crowd continued to turn up their noses, waiting to see the more serious paintings. Still the auctioneer solicited, "The son! The son! Who will take the son?

No one wanted "the Son." Only one person – the young soldier who painted it – bid $10. The crowd impatiently cried out in unison, "Sell it to him and let's get on with the auction." The auctioneer pounded the gavel and sold the painting for the bid of $10.

To everyone's consternation the auctioneer closed the auction. The hostile crowd demanded to know how after coming all this way could the auction possibly be over.

The auctioneer explained a stipulation in the will. According to the wishes of the deceased, the painting of the son was to be sold first and whoever took the son would "get it all," the art collection as well as the entire estate. The crowd sat in stunned silence staring at the young soldier.

The point of the story is simple. Whoever takes the son gets it all! That is the point of the Christian story. Remember it now and forevermore.

See the eternal "Inheritance" in the words of the Apostle Peter. "Blessed be the God and Father of our Lord Jesus Christ! By his great mercy he has given us a new birth into a living hope through the resurrection of Jesus Christ from the dead, and into an inheritance that is imperishable, undefiled, and unfading, kept in heaven for you, who are being protected by the power of God through faith for a salvation ready to be revealed in the last time." 1 Peter 1:3-9

Sing and/or Listen

"My faith looks up to Thee"
https://www.youtube.com/watch?v=oGKLm-ThF2to

Pray

Holy God, I/we celebrate the resurrection of Jesus Christ. Because the King is alive, we are set free from the power of sin and death. Through him, like so many others, I also experience new and resurrected life. Fears and anxieties no longer hold me in their grip. By your Spirit, embolden me/us to live courageously and faithfully to the truth of Jesus' Resurrection. Amen.

The Spiritual Discipline of Journaling

A way to concentrate on being in God's presence.

1. Read the selected scripture passage. Record your immediate thoughts.

2. Read the devotion/reflection for today. Record your thoughts and/or write your personal reflections.

3. Prayerfully listen for God's message to you. Record what you hear from the Lord.

4. Pray the prayer that is written and/or record and pray your own prayer.

5. Conclude with praise and worship. Use the suggested hymn from YouTube or choose another.

Friday

"The Witnesses"
Acts 2:14a, 22-32

2:14a "But Peter, standing with the eleven, raised his voice and addressed them . . . 2:32 'This Jesus God raised up, and of that all of us are witnesses.'"

Laurence Stallings was a film writer during the first quarter of the last century. He accepted an unusual assignment to cover a football game between the University of Pennsylvania and the University of Illinois. The year was 1925. The brilliant halfback Red Grange gave a dazzling performance as he broke loose on the muddy field for three touchdowns and set up a fourth. Stallings was in a tizzy as he tried to put the story into words. He paced up and down the press box with his hands clasped to his head. "I can't," he exclaimed, "I can't write it! It's too big."

The story of the resurrection of Jesus is like that. It's too big to write. It's bigger than Donald Trump and Making America Great Again. Bigger, too, than Bill Gates and Microsoft. Bigger, too, than Steve Jobs and Apple, Mark Zuckerberg and Facebook, Craig Newmark and Craigslist, Sergey Brin/Larry Page and Google.

The resurrection of Jesus is the pivotal event of human history. It is the most sensational story of human existence.

As Peter said, "God raised him up, having freed him from death, because it was impossible for him to be held in its power." Acts 2:24

That's why the bells are ringing
And drums are drumming
And resurrection-people are dancing
Because Jesus is still Jesus!

And that's why feet are stomping
And doves are flying

And bands are marching
And fingers are snapping,
And tongues are praising
And hands are clapping
And trumpets are blaring
And choirs are singing
And cymbals are clashing
And children are laughing!
Because Jesus is still alive!

And that's why eyes are smiling
And knees are kneeling
And banners are flowing
And horns are blowing
And voices are singing
And crowds are cheering!
Because Jesus is the Risen Christ!

And that's why arms are waving,
Tambourines are playing,
Choirs are singing,
Hearts are humming,
Old men are running!
Because Jesus is our Resurrected Lord,

Christ is present now and will always be

present.
Believe it until the shaking quits,
Believe it until the thunder stops rolling,
Believe it until the lightening stops flashing,
Believe it until the midnight of despair
Turns into the glorious sunrise of hope.

With a faith like that
Nothing and no one can stop you.
For you won't give up, shut up, let up,
until you had stayed up, stored up, prayed up,
paid up,
and given Christ the glory.

Whatever else happens, the Lord Jesus Christ is
present with us as we live through the storms.
To him be all honor and glory, now and
forevermore!

Nothing and no one can stop you.
For you won't give up, shut up, let up,
until you had stayed up, stored up, prayed up,
paid up,
and given Christ the glory.

Whatever else happens, the Lord Jesus Christ is present with us as we live through the storms. To him be all honor and glory, now and forevermore! Amen & Amen!

Sing and/or Listen

"Christ Be Beside Me"

https://www.youtube.com/watch?v=0BGug-Mak4ys

Pray

King Jesus, my Lord and Savior, be near me, just as you were near to the disciples. Not only me but also be near to each and every one who confesses your name and looks forward to that day when you return and your glory fills the sky for everyone to see. Amen

The Spiritual Discipline of Journaling

A way to concentrate on being in God's presence.

1. Read the selected scripture passage. Record your immediate thoughts.

2. Read the devotion/reflection for today. Record your thoughts and/or write your personal reflections.

3. Prayerfully listen for God's message to you. Record what you hear from the Lord.

4. Pray the prayer that is written and/or record and pray your own prayer.

5. Conclude with praise and worship. Use the suggested hymn from YouTube or choose another.

Saturday

John 20:26-31

"Thomas said, 'I will not believe until I see. ...' Jesus came and stood among them and said, 'Peace be with you.' Then he said to Thomas, 'Put your finger here and see my hands. Reach out your hand and put it in my side. Do not doubt but believe.' Thomas answered him, 'My Lord and my God!'"

"Doubting Thomas"

There's a wonderful painting of this gospel scene in which Jesus presents his side for Thomas to touch. The painting is entitled "Doubting Thomas."

In this picture Jesus lets Thomas get up close to see his wounds. Thomas is bent over, eye level with the wound in Jesus' side and Jesus is guiding his hand so that he might feel the wound for himself. You can almost hear Jesus gently saying to Thomas, "Now, reach out your hand and put it in my side. Do not doubt, but believe." And in the painting Thomas' finger is buried in the gaping hole in Jesus' side all the way up to the knuckle. In the painting, Thomas does what so many of us would like to do, he pokes around in Jesus' wounds, he looks and touches so that he might verify for himself that this is indeed the Risen Lord

After that, Thomas was fully convinced that Christ was alive. When Jesus held out his hands and showed his side to Thomas it was for a purpose - so that he might believe. And Thomas replied, "My Lord and My God." Then Jesus said, "Because you have seen me you have believed; blessed are those who have not seen and yet have believed."

That includes us. We were not there with Thomas and the other disciples. We cannot touch the Lord's risen body, as they did; nevertheless, we believe he is alive.

Yes, that faith is blessing. We are blessed, not because we are so intelligent but simply because of faith in his resurrection.

Sing and/or Listen!

https://www.youtube.com/watch?v=wcE9-An-goeM

Through it all, through it all,
Oh I've learned to trust in Jesus,
I've learned to trust in God.
Through it all, through it all
I've learned to depend on his Word.
United Methodist Hymnal Number 507

Pray

Dear Jesus, our Lord and King, we confess your resurrection. Forgive us for any vestige of doubt and us to be stronger in faith. I believe, help thou my unbelief. Amen.

The Spiritual Discipline of Journaling

A way to concentrate on being in God's presence.

1. Read the selected scripture passage. Record your immediate thoughts.

2. Read the devotion/reflection for today. Record your thoughts and/or write your personal reflections.

3. Prayerfully listen for God's message to you. Record what you hear from the Lord.

4. Pray the prayer that is written and/or record and pray your own prayer.

5. Conclude with praise and worship. Use the suggested hymn from YouTube or choose another.

THE SECOND SUNDAY OF EASTER

John 20:26-31

"A week later his disciples were again in the house, and Thomas was with them. Although the doors were shut, Jesus came and stood among them and said, 'Peace be with you.' Then he said to Thomas, 'Put your finger here and see my hands. Reach out your hand and put it in my side. Do not doubt but believe.' Thomas answered him, 'My Lord and my God!' Jesus said to him, 'Have you believed because you have seen me? Blessed are those who have not seen and yet have come to believe.' Now Jesus did many other signs in the presence of his disciples, which are not written in this book. But these are written so that you may come to believe that Jesus is the Messiah, the Son of God, and that through believing you may have life in his name."

"Blessed"

"Blessed are those who have not seen and yet have come to believe." Focus on the words of Jesus to Doubting Thomas.

Is it really true? Are those who believe in the resurrection of Jesus Christ truly blessed?

Yes! Of course! This resurrection faith lives within and blesses us now.

• Through the storm and through the rain, belief in the resurrection of Jesus sustains us.

• Through the good times and the bad, belief in the resurrection of Jesus sustains us.

• When the death angel arrives and takes some home, belief in the resurrection of Jesus sustains us.

• When climbing up the rough side of the mountain, belief in the resurrection of Jesus sustains us.

• When the parents weep for a dying child, belief in the resurrection of Jesus sustains us.

• When the thunder clears her throat in the heavens, and the lightening rips across the midnight sky, belief in the resurrection of Jesus sustains us.

Belief in the resurrection of Jesus will not work magic, however. It will not put money in bank accounts, for example, or suddenly deliver from alcohol/food/sexual addictions, or delete one's criminal history, or save one's marriage.

Jesus looked into the eyes of "doubting Thomas' and said "Blessed are those who have not seen and yet have come to believe." Is it true? Indeed! This is the Word of the Lord!

Those who believe in the resurrection of Jesus Christ are truly blessed by their faith in his resurrection.

53

Sing and/or Listen
https://www.youtube.com/watch?v=YSf1VABM
N1s
"I Know Whom I Have Believed"
I know not why God's wondrous grace
To me He hath made known,
Nor why, unworthy, Christ in love
Redeemed me for His own.

Pray

Lord Jesus, open my eyes that I may see you.
Help me grow in faith and continue to believe
that you are alive and among us. Reinforce
within my mind and heart the good news of your
resurrection. Amen.

The Spiritual Discipline of Journaling

A way to concentrate on being in God's presence.

1. Read the selected scripture passage. Record your immediate thoughts.

2. Read the devotion/reflection for today. Record your thoughts and/or write your personal reflections.

3. Prayerfully listen for God's message to you. Record what you hear from the Lord.

4. Pray the prayer that is written and/or record and pray your own prayer.

5. Conclude with praise and worship. Use the suggested hymn from YouTube or choose another.

Monday

Luke 17:11-19

"On the way to Jerusalem Jesus was going through the region between Samaria and Galilee. As he entered a village, ten lepers approached him. Keeping their distance, they called out, saying, 'Jesus, Master, have mercy on us!' When he saw them, he said to them, 'Go and show yourselves to the priests.' And as they went, they were made clean. Then one of them, when he saw that he was healed, turned back, praising God with a loud voice. He prostrated himself at Jesus' feet and thanked him. And he was a Samaritan. Then Jesus asked, 'Were not ten made clean? But the other nine, where are they? Was none of them found to return and give praise to God except this foreigner?' Then he said to him, 'Get up and go on your way; your faith has made you well.'"

"Ten Lepers"

There were ten lepers. Then there was only one. What happened to the other nine? Why did they not come back to Jesus? Who knows? It is hard to understand people like that, who don't take the time and expend the energy to acknowledge and praise God for the blessings received from God's hands.

Only one leper returned to give thanks for this great healing which happened in his life. He was healed-up, stirred-up, worked-up, dialed-up, prayed-up, lit-up, and signed-up to give God the glory. "He . . . praised God," says the gospel text, and "he prostrated himself at the feet of Jesus and thanked him." Jesus said to the leper, "Rise and go your way; your faith has made you well."

Don't overlook the power of faith. The truth is that even a small faith is boost-you-up motor power. Faith will perk you up, pick you up, pump you up, push you up, and put your feet on solid ground. Faith will take you from where you are to where you ought to be. Faith is your ticket out of the nightmare room into the safe room, out of the sick room into the healing room. There is no song so broken, no monotone so horrible, no voice so tremulous, no life so broken, that God

57

can't take it and compose it into a beautiful symphony.

Jesus said, "Your faith has made you well." Of course! Will we, like the Leper, take the time to return to Jesus to thank him and praise God for the blessings of healing?

Sing and/or listen!
"Thank You, Lord"
https://www.youtube.com/watch?v=H4DIFtN9
9FI

Pray

Dear Jesus, I join all who celebrate your victory over death and the power of sin. The empty cross and the empty tomb witness to hope in our broken world. I pray for all who, like the leper, give thanks for healing in their life. Moreover, I pray for all who suffer in mind, body or spirit, and who lack the strength or faith to give thanks. I offer thanks on their behalf. Have mercy! Amen.

The Spiritual Discipline of Journaling

A way to concentrate on being in God's presence.

1. Read the selected scripture passage. Record your immediate thoughts.

2. Read the devotion/reflect on for today. Record your thoughts and/or write your personal reflections.

3. Prayerfully listen for God's message to you. Record what you hear from the Lord.

4. Pray the prayer that is written and/or record and pray your own prayer.

5. Conclude with praise and worship. Use the suggested hymn from YouTube or choose another.

Tuesday

Luke 7:36-50

"One of the Pharisees asked Jesus to eat with him, and he went into the Pharisee's house and took his place at the table. And a woman in the city, who was a sinner, having learned that he was eating in the Pharisee's house, brought an alabaster jar of ointment. She stood behind him at his feet, weeping, and began to bathe his feet with her tears and to dry them with her hair. Then she continued kissing his feet and anointing them with the ointment. Now when the Pharisee who had invited him saw it, he said to himself, 'If this man were a prophet, he would have known who and what kind of woman this is who is touching him—that she is a sinner.' Jesus spoke up and said to him, 'Simon, I have something to say to you.' . . . I tell you, her sins, which were many, have been forgiven; hence she has shown great love. . ..' Then he said to her, 'Your sins are forgiven." . . .' And he said to the woman, 'Your faith has saved you; go in peace.

"The Risen Christ and Flawed People"

The gospel is bursting with stories of Jesus and flawed people. Think of Zacchaeus, Matthew, Peter, etcetera, and this story of the woman of the night who dried Jesus feet with her hair. No question about her history. Everyone knew her story. She was a flawed person. Nevertheless, she responded enthusiastically to Jesus Christ. She loved him so much because he forgave her so much.

This story took place when Jesus was a guest in the house of Simon, a highly respected religious leader in the city. The evening meal was being served. Suddenly, to everyone's surprise, this "woman of the city, a sinner," to quote the gospel story, crashed the party, and began to lavish affection on Jesus. She was so emotional that her tears drenched his body. She dried him off with her long hair and anointed his body with very expensive oil. She truly loved the Lord.

Why is that? Why would a flawed person like that love Christ so much? Because he had treated her with such profound respect and love, as a person who counts rather than a person to be counted, as a person made in the image of God. He honored her God-given dignity. He was God's grace to her, the undeserved, unearned and loving action of God in her life. He absolved her sins.

Do you understand this woman and her over-the-top affection for Jesus? Do I? Does anyone? Let all who do, joyfully sing Bill Gather's song.

Sing and/or listen
"He Touched Me"
https://www.youtube.com/watch?v=4HSW
TAZZUB8
Pray
Heavenly Father, I have been redeemed, set free, and given new life! Thank you, Lord, for your grace and mercy through King Jesus. Amen.

Wednesday

Luke 18:9-14

"To some who were confident of their own right-eousness and looked down on everybody else, Jesus told this parable: 'Two men went up to the temple to pray, one a Pharisee and the other a tax collector. The Pharisee stood up and prayed about[a] himself: 'God, I thank you that I am not like other men—robbers, evildoers, adulterers—or even like this tax collector. I fast twice a week and give a tenth of all I get.' But the tax collector stood at a distance. He would not even look up to heaven, but beat his breast and said, 'God, have mercy on me, a sinner.' I tell you that this man, rather than the other, went home justified before God. For everyone who exalts himself will be humbled, and he who humbles himself will be exalted.'"

"Good News for Flawed People"

It is true. Isn't it? When we go to church we hear about God's mercy. And it doesn't matter whether the church is Protestant or Catholic or

Orthodox. We hear it at United Methodist, Baptist, Presbyterian, Episcopal, Catholic and Orthodox churches. We have heard it at our local church as well as at St. Peter's Basilica in Rome, at the National Cathedral in Washington as well as Canterbury in London. Wherever we attend a Christian church, we hear "God's mercy" spoken.

God's mercy is the heart of the great hymns, prayers, liturgy, and preaching of the church. That's good news for all of us who have sinned and fallen short of the glory of God. And, in today's gospel, Christ opens to us this great mercy of God for flawed people.

We are more broken and sinful than we could ever imagine. In contrast to that, here is the good news: we are more loved and cherished than we could ever dare hope.

Which do we choose, to focus on how broken we are or how much we are loved and cherished by our Lord Jesus Christ?

Does anyone remember that Dennis the Menace cartoon from some years back? As you know, Dennis is indeed a menace to his next-door neighbors, Mr. and Mrs. Wilson, and yet

Mrs. Wilson continues to be kind and gracious because that is her nature. This particular cartoon shows Dennis and his little friend Joey leaving Mrs. Wilson's house, their hands full of cookies. Joey says, "I wonder what we did to deserve this." Dennis answers, and his answer is on target: "Look, Joey, Mrs. Wilson gives us cookies not because we're nice, but because she's nice."

That's also true in a religious sense – Jesus Christ cherishes us, not because we're nice but because he's nice. Likewise, God is merciful to the tax collector and all sorts of broken people, not because they suddenly become nice and respectable but because God is by nature a loving and merciful God.

Let us acknowledge and confess our personal brokenness to be sure but refuse to stop there. Rather, moved on and focus on how much we are cherished by the living Christ.

Pray
Lord have mercy on me, a sinner. Amen

Sing and/or listen
"O Love That Wilt Not Let Me Go"
https://www.youtube.com/watch?v=XyqV-
APfc9I

The Spiritual Discipline of Journaling

1. Read the selected scripture passage.
Record your immediate thoughts.

2. Read the devotion/reflection for today.
Record your thoughts and/or write your personal reflections.

3. Prayerfully listen for God's message to you.
Record what you hear from the Lord.

4. Compose and pray your own prayer.

5. Conclude with praise and worship. Use the suggested hymn from YouTube or choose another.

Thursday

Luke 24:33-49

"Then he (Jesus) said to them . . . 'Thus it is written, that the Messiah is to suffer and to rise from
the dead on the third day, and that repentance
and forgiveness of sins is to be proclaimed in his
name to all nations, beginning from Jerusalem. .
.'"

"No Limits on Divine Forgiveness"

David Berkowitz, known as the Son of Sam,
killed six people and wounded seven in a year-
long killing rampage in the New York City envi-
rons. That sparked one of the biggest manhunts
in the history of New York. David was sentenced
to over 300 years with no hope of parole ever.

Even after ten years into his prison sentence,
he was constantly in trouble, a persistent disci-
plinary problem. He really had a bad attitude.
Then, one night as he was walking the prison
yard, another inmate said to him, "Listen, I know

you're David Berkowitz, and I want to tell you something." The inmate said, "I want you to know that Jesus Christ loves you. . .." David said to the inmate, "I've done too many evil things and there's no forgiveness for me. Maybe there's a God out there someplace, but I don't think he has any interest in me at all." The inmate would not back off. He said, "No, you're wrong. David, God . . . can forgive you."

That started a friendship between the two prisoners. "And" said David, "we would meet in the yard, and we would walk around together, and he started to share Christ with me. And within a couple of months' time he led me to the Lord."

David Berkowitz said in his interview with Scott Ross, "I know no matter what man may say, I know what God has done for me. That he has reached into my life, and he's taken out that rotten heart of a murderer, of a devil worshiper, a heart that was no good. It was like a stone! I was like an animal! I was like a rock! And he's taken that thing out and put in a new heart and a new

68

spirit within me, that I can praise the name of Jesus today, and I thank God for that."

Shocking that even David Berkowitz was eligible for divine forgiveness. Is that what Jesus intended when he said to his disciples in the Upper Room, that "repentance and forgiveness of sins is to be proclaimed in his name to all nations."

Yes, of course! The bottom line is that Christ the King did not and has not to this day placed restrictions on divine forgiveness of sins.

Sing and/or listen
"Just as I Am"

https://www.youtube.com/watch?v=_gGBMv4 2dJY

Pray

Dear Lord, be merciful to me. I have sinned and fallen short. Thank you for your grace. Amen.

The Spiritual Discipline of Journaling

A way to concentrate on being in God's presence.

1. Read the selected scripture passage. Record your immediate thoughts.

2. Read the devotion/reflection for today. Record your thoughts and/or write your personal reflections.

3. Prayerfully listen for God's message to you. Record what you hear from the Lord.

4. Pray the prayer that is written and/or record and pray your own prayer.

5. Conclude with praise and worship. Use the suggested hymn from YouTube or choose another.

Friday

"What are the limits to John 3:16?"

"For God so loved the world that he gave his only Son, so that everyone who believes in him may not perish but may have eternal life."

The Reflection

Aaron Hernandez's Hernandez, the former tight end for the New England Patriots, had been serving a life sentence without parole after being convicted in the June 2013 murder of Odin Lloyd. He was found dead with the Bible verse, "John 3:16," written on his forehead. Most Christians know the words, "For God so loved the world that he gave his only Son, so that everyone who believes in him may not perish but may have eternal life."

According to the joint statement from law enforcement, Hernandez was locked in his cell about 8 p.m. on Tuesday night, and no one entered the cell until he was found by a correction officer at 3:03 a.m. He was taken to a hospital and pronounced dead about an hour later.

71

Investigators officially ruled his death a suicide and released new details about the circumstances of his hanging on Thursday.

Hernandez's death came just five days after his acquittal in the 2012 slayings of two men outside a Boston nightclub in a separate case.

Why did he do it? Why did Aaron write "John 3:16" on his forehead? Did he really believe? Who knows?

Here's the question, do you/do I believe that "God so loved the world that he gave his only Son, so that everyone who believes in him may not perish but may have eternal life."

Where do you draw the line on God's grace and mercy? More importantly, where does God draw the line?

Listen and/or Sing!
Amazing grace! how sweet the sound
https://www.youtube.com/watch?v=HsCp5LG_zNE

Pray

Lord, thank you for your grace and mercy.
Amazing grace! How sweet the sound! Amen

72

The Spiritual Discipline of Journaling

A way to concentrate on being in God's presence.

1. Read the selected scripture passage. Record your immediate thoughts.

2. Read the devotion/reflection for today. Record your thoughts and/or write your personal reflections.

3. Prayerfully listen for God's message to you. Record what you hear from the Lord.

4. Pray the prayer that is written and/or record and pray your own prayer.

5. Conclude with praise and worship. Use the suggested hymn from YouTube or choose another.

Saturday

Romans 5:1-8

"But God proves his love for us in that while we still were sinners Christ died for us." (v.8)

"God's Love"

The Associated press issued a human-interest story regarding Arnold Palmer, following his surgery in '99. He was playing in his last tournament before undergoing follow-up radiation therapy for prostate cancer. The story stated that he was pleased by the outpouring of affection and encouragement expressed by his fans in the Fred Meyer Challenge. Verbal get-well wishes were presented by his fans at every hole during the first round. And as the golfer approached the first tee of the two-day charity event, a fan exclaimed, "Arnold Palmer, God love you, sir."[1]

There's no question about it. That's not a statement about Arnold Palmer but about God. Without doubt, God loves every person. That's the one thing we can count on in this world. The Bible clearly teaches that God is love and loves every human being, sinners as well as saints. See it there in the scripture words. "But God proves his love for us in that while we still were sinners Christ died for us."

There you have the truth of it encapsulated in one short verse of the New Testament: the abiding, eternal love of God the Father. Amen.

---

[1] 1.54 a.m. ET (555 GMT) August 25, 1998 ALOHA, Ore. (AP)

Sing and/or Listen

"The Love of God"

https://www.youtube.com/watch?v=nEi463
LcxxA

Pray

Holy God, your love is a mystery that is incom-
prehensible to me. It welcomes me, even me,
into your presence. Because of the good news of
your love, I dare to hope for eternal life with you.
Thank you for loving even me and forgiving my
sins. Amen.

The Spiritual Discipline of Journaling

A way to concentrate on being in God's presence.

1. Read the selected scripture passage. Record your immediate thoughts.

2. Read the devotion/reflection for today. Record your thoughts and/or write your personal reflections.

3. Prayerfully listen for God's message to you. Record what you hear from the Lord.

4. Pray the prayer that is written and/or record and pray your own prayer.

5. Conclude with praise and worship. Use the suggested hymn from YouTube or choose another.

THE THIRD SUNDAY OF EASTER

Celebrate! He is Lord!

Luke 24:13-49

"Now on that same day two of them were going to a village called Emmaus, about seven miles from Jerusalem, and talking with each other about all these things that had happened. While they were talking and discussing, Jesus himself came near and went with them . . .. They got up and returned to Jerusalem; and they found the eleven and their companions gathered together. They were saying, 'The Lord has risen indeed, and he has appeared to Simon!' Then they told what had happened on the road, and how he had been made known to them in the breaking of the bread. While they were talking about this, Jesus himself stood among them and said to them, 'Peace be with you.' They were startled and terrified, and thought that they were seeing

78

a ghost. He said to them, 'Why are you frightened, and why do doubts arise in your hearts? Look at my hands and my feet; see that it is I myself. Touch me and see; for a ghost does not have flesh and bones as you see that I have.' And when he had said this, he showed them his hands and his feet. While in their joy they were disbelieving and still wondering, he said to them, 'Have you anything here to eat?'"

"He Stood Among Them"

Talk about disheartened, dismayed, downcast, and defeated disciples! There they are in the gospel story. Clearly, they are a picture of beaten, crushed, despondent, dejected human beings. They were mixed up, snarled up, fouled up, messed up, mucked up, and baled—up. They had been through Good Friday, a gut-wrenching event causing them mental and emotional anguish. They were like people desperate for mood altering medications. They stood still, their faces downcast. (v 17).

It is precisely at this point of their despair that Christ joined two of them on the road to Emmaus and the others later in the Upper Room. As the gospel acknowledges, they had questions – serious questions, too – about the resurrection of Jesus Christ. And, of course, questions linger to this very day. While the church has settled that question for Christianity, many Christians still have questions about what really happened to Jesus.

The answer is not found in science. We know that NASA engineers, aeronautical scientists, and teachers can lay out the steps for the journey to the moon and back, but not for the journey of Christ from death back to life.

The fact is that this road to Emmaus and the Upper Room stories are very strange because Jesus who died on Good Friday is pictured as talking to his disciples. Indeed, this is bizarre to non-Christian people living today on planet earth.

Jesus died on Good Friday. Then, to everyone's surprise, he showed up in the Upper

Room on Easter Sunday and proved his resurrection to his disciples. So, we sing with confidence: "He is Lord."

Sing and/or Listen

https://www.youtube.com/watch?v=ujznyzGoQ0w

Pray

I thank you, Heavenly Father, for the fact of Christ the King's resurrection. As I face the reality of death, remind me to stop, listen, and hear the voice of Jesus say, "Do not be afraid; fear not, for I am with you always, even to the end of time." Moreover, I choose to rejoice that my risen Lord is with me/us now and forever. Amen.

The Spiritual Discipline of Journaling

A way to concentrate on being in God's presence.

1. Read the selected scripture passage. Record your immediate thoughts.

2. Read the devotion/reflection for today. Record your thoughts and/or write your personal reflections.

3. Prayerfully listen for God's message to you. Record what you hear from the Lord.

4. Pray the prayer that is written and/or record and pray your own prayer.

5. Conclude with praise and worship. Use the suggested hymn from YouTube or choose another.

Monday

"Does God rea ly care?

I Peter 1:18-21

"You know that you were ransomed from the fu-
tile ways inherited from your ancestors, not with
perishable things like silver or gold, but with the
precious blood of Christ, like that of a lamb without defect or blemish. He was destined before
the foundation of the world, but was revealed at
the end of the ages for your sake. Through him
you have come to trust in God, who raised him
from the dead and gave him glory, so that your
faith and hope are set on God."

"Connecting the Dots"

She asked me a question. "What is it that
God has never seen?" Well, she had me on that
one. After all, God sees and knows all things.
Nothing escapes his sight. "Alright," I said,

83

"you've got me. What is it that God has not seen?" "His equal," she replied. "God has never seen his equal!"

It's true. Isn't it? God has not seen God's equal. Neither have I. Nevertheless, God sent God's Son to the Holy Land for the salvation of the world. "Through him," to use the words of I Peter, "you have come to trust in God, who raised him from the dead and gave him glory, so that your faith and hope are set on God."

"Does God really care about us/me?" The answer is yes. The evidence for it is not good health, or wealth, or family, or country. Conversely, poor health or poverty or a dysfunctional family or the death of a child or the loss of a job are not signs that God does not care.

"Does God really care about us/me?" We know God cares because of God's gift of Jesus and the incorporation of us into God's mighty acts of salvation. The manger, the cross, the empty tomb, and the Holy Sacraments are the historical and present-day evidence of God's loving care for each one of us.

"For God so loved the world that he gave his only Son, so that everyone who believes in him may not perish but may have eternal life."

Sing and/or Listen

"Because He lives"
https://www.youtube.com/watch?v=spa7Wkwj
wGw

Pray

Heavenly Father, in the resurrection of King Jesus the dots are connected. Help me to trust this good news. Unclutter my mind from all confusions. Teach me how to get to clarity and to go on, step by little step, trusting his mercy and grace. I choose to live in the light of Christ's resurrection and to be free of fear and free for life. Amen.

The Spiritual Discipline of Journaling

1. Read the selected scripture passage. Record your immediate thoughts.

2. Read the devotion/reflection for today. Record your thoughts and/or write your personal reflections.

3. Prayerfully listen for God's message to you. Record what you hear from the Lord.

4. Pray the prayer that is written and/or record and pray your own prayer.

5. Conclude with praise and worship. Use the suggested hymn from YouTube or choose another.

Tuesday

1 Peter 2:19-25

"Christ also suffered for you, . . .When he was abused, he did not return abuse; when he suffered, he did not threaten; but he entrusted himself to the one who judges justly. He himself bore our sins in his body on the cross, so that, free from sins, we might live for righteousness; by his wounds you have been healed. For you were going astray like sheep, but you have returned to the shepherd and guardian of your souls."

"The Shepherd and Guardian of Our souls"

Imagine that – the Shepherd and Guardian of your soul. What an image! I have not dreamed it up; rather, it is an image of Jesus from the gospel and the epistle.

• Through the storm and through the rain, focus on the Shepherd and Guardian of your soul
• Through the good times and the bad, focus on

the Shepherd and Guardian of your soul.
• When death takes your loved one, focus on the Shepherd and Guardian of your soul.
• When climbing up the rough side of the mountain, focus on the Shepherd and Guardian of your soul.
• When you fear for your children, focus on the Shepherd and Guardian of your soul.
• When the thunder clears her throat in the heavens and the lightening rips across the midnight sky, focus on the Shepherd and Guardian of your soul.
• Whatever happens, focus on the Shepherd and Guardian of your soul. We don't have to agree.
• Whatever happens, focus on the Shepherd and Guardian of your soul. We can respect one another.
• Whatever happens, focus the Shepherd and Guardian of your soul. We can be civil.
• Whatever happens, focus on the Shepherd and Guardian of your soul. We can be courteous.

Jesus is the Shepherd and Guardian of your soul. Stop whatever you are doing, bow your head, and visualize this image of the Shepherd and Guardian of your soul. That is the reality in the good days and the bad. Praise God!

Sing and/or Listen

"The King of Love
My Shepherd Is"

https://www.youtube.com/watch?v=jfx
f4YMYd1k

The King of love my shepherd is,
Whose goodness faileth never;
I nothing lack if
And he is mine forever.

And so through all the length of days
Thy goodness faileth never.
Good Shepherd, may I sing thy praise
Within thy house forever.

- The United Methodist Hymnal Number 138

Pray

Jesus, Good Shepherd, I choose to focus on you at all times and in all places. Have mercy on me and help to stay focused. Amen.

The Spiritual Discipline of Journaling

1. Read the selected scripture passage. Record your immediate thoughts.

2. Read the devotion/reflection for today. Record your thoughts and/or write your personal reflections.

3. Prayerfully listen for God's message to you. Record what you hear from the Lord.

4. Pray the prayer that is written and/or record and pray your own prayer.

5. Conclude with praise and worship. Use the suggested hymn from YouTube or choose another.

Wednesday

"The Lord is my shepherd"

Palm 23

What is ahead of us? We do not know whether the days will be good or bad. But the one thing present day Christians believe is, "The Lord is my shepherd."

Thumbs up on that awesome truth. It is the dominate note of the Bible, the unwavering conviction of the prophets, the underlying assumption of the gospel. The Lord will not fail. In the Lord there is no weakness, no wobbling, and no disguised brittleness. You can be sure that the Lord will endure everything and still be "my/your shepherd" at the of the day and the end of life.

That is the point. Isn't it? The world can change around us. Terrorists can hijack and crash American Airplanes into the World Trade Center. Tornadoes, hurricanes and floods can disrupt and destroy cities as well as the countryside. Everything can collapse in the social order so that

91

everyone is vulnerable. But the Lord is still the Lord. Nothing can change the fact of that.

The Lord was the Lord a million years ago. The Lord was the Lord all day yesterday. The Lord is the Lord all day today. The Lord will be the Lord all day tomorrow. The Lord will be the Lord after time has long since disappeared. The Lord is my Shepherd.

You can count on the Lord, put your whole trust in his loving care. Whatever the outward circumstance, "the Lord is my shepherd." That's the faith that has kept Christians going in the midst of wars and bloodshed, persecution and revolution, political corruption and upheaval, life and death. You can depend on it, too, put your whole trust in it and count on the Lord forever.

This faith, "the Lord is my shepherd," will keep you going in a world of risk. Who can you trust? What if you lost everything? Can you count on your broker? Can you trust your HMO? Is your phone service ripping you off? Who will look after your 401(k)? Will you end up like that retiree who ran out of money and spent eleven years sweeping floors at the Burger King Store?

Everything is at risk. Nevertheless, "the Lord is my shepherd."

"God Will Take Care of You"

Sing and or Listen

https://www.youtube.com/watch?v=MdZ7RdF07Eo

Be not dismayed whatever betide
God will take care of you
Beneath His wings of love abide
God will take care of you
God will take care of you
Through everyday o'er all the way
He will care for you
God will take care of you
- The United Methodist Church Hymnal

Pray

Lord, help me to stop and trust you for my life. So much is beyond my control. Yet, you are here and I want to trust you. Have mercy on me. Amen

---

The Spiritual Discipline of Journaling

1. Read the selected scripture passage. Record your immediate thoughts.

2. Read the devotion/reflection for today. Record your thoughts and/or write your personal reflections.

3. Prayerfully listen for God's message to you. Record what you hear from the Lord.

4. Pray the prayer that is written and/or record and pray your own prayer.

5. Conclude with praise and worship. Use the suggested hymn from YouTube or choose another.

Friday

"We are never alone!"
"Yea, though I walk through the valley of the shadow of death, I will fear no evil: for thou art with me; thy rod and thy staff they comfort me." Palm 23:4

"Never alone!"

As we move forward into the next chapter of our valley of transition, we are confident that we are never alone. Our Shepherd is with us.

Whatever happens to us, we are not alone. The reality is that the Lord makes me, leads me, and restores me.

• Through storm and through rain, the Lord is with us!

• And even if catastrophe strikes, the Lord is with us!

• And even if the world crumbles around us and life falls apart, the Lord is with us!

In the transition time we will never have to stand alone. The Lord will be there. The reality is that the Lord makes me, leads me, and restores me.

• If cancer invades my body, He will be there.

• And if we are shut out, locked out, kept out, pushed out, punched out, and left out, the Lord will be there.

• And if addiction takes us down, He will be there.

• And if we are shut out, locked out, kept out, pushed out, punched out, and left out, the Lord will be there.

The Lord is with us! The Lord makes me lie down in green pastures, leads me beside the still waters, and restores me

• When men won't do right, He will be there.

• When there is fear, shame, rejection, and isolation, He will be there.

• When the heavens weep, the seas and rivers flood, He will be there.

• When the thunder clears her throat in the heavens, He will be here.

The Lord is with us during transition! The reality is that the Lord makes me lie down in green pastures, leads me beside the still waters, and restores me

• When you are compelled to change the past and desperate to stop the future, He will be there.

• When in love you teach your children everything you know and they still go wrong, He will be here.

• In a world of geniuses, crackpots, dictators, simpletons, and terrorists, He is here.

The Lord is with us through transition! The reality is that the Lord makes me, leads me, and restores me.

• When there are rumors and suspicions and questions unanswered, He is here.

• When you are confused and doubtful and your soul is searching for answers, He is here.

• When it is so hard to build trust and so easy to break it, He is here.

• When no one seems to understand the power of a promise and lets you down, He is here.

The Lord is with us. The reality is that the Lord makes us, leads us, and restores us.

• We have unlimited access to the Lord's love,

• And unlimited access to a network that has

97

been established at a great price,
• And unlimited access to a 24 hour a day tech support,
•And unlimited access to training,
• And unlimited access to answers and resources just around the corner.

 The Lord is with us. The reality is that the Lord makes me, leads me, and restores me. Praise the Lord!

"Immanuel - God is with us"
Sing and/or Listen
https://www.youtube.com/watch?v=KEDhl
vs4BdI

Pray

 I welcome you, precious Immanuel to my journey this day. I dedicate my life to your glory and honor. Help me to lift high your name, to praise you, to proclaim your kingdom and to be renewed again as your disciple. To you be blessing and majesty and power, wisdom and glory and might, now and forevermore. Amen!

The Spiritual Discipline of Journaling

1. Read the selected scripture passage. Record your immediate thoughts.

2. Read the devotion/reflection for today. Record your thoughts and/or write your personal reflections.

3. Prayerfully listen for God's message to you. Record what you hear from the Lord.

4. Pray the prayer that is written and/or record and pray your own prayer.

5. Conclude with praise and worship. Use the suggested hymn from YouTube or choose another.

Saturday

"I Will Fear no Evil"
"Yea, though I walk through the valley of the shadow of death, I will fear no evil: for thou art with me; thy rod and thy staff they comfort me."
Palm 23:4

"I Fear no Evil"

I am confident that the Lord is my ever-present-shepherd. "I fear no evil."

• I do not say "I fear no evil" because I have a burglarproof and an infallible security system in my home.

• I do not say, ""I fear no evil" because the government and the military can protect me from terrorist who wish to do me harm.

• I do not say "I fear no evil" because I am protected from sickness, or heart attacks, or death.

I say "I fear no evil" because "the Lord is my Shepherd."

"I fear no evil."

- Not in the valley of death,
- Not in the valley of doubt,
- Not in the valley of illness.
- Not in the valley of transition.

Why not? Because "the Lord is my shepherd" and is "with me." Yes! Right now, and right here.

Well, whether I can confidently say "I will not fear because you are with me," the good news is "God with me." That is the meaning of Emmanuel. "God is with us." Even if I find it hard to believe, "the Lord is my shepherd" and is still with me.

We don't know what lies ahead of us. We do not know whether the days will be good or bad. But one thing we do know: "my/your shepherd" is with us and holds us in his heart.

As Job said (19:25-27), "I know that my Redeemer lives, and that at the last he will stand upon the earth; and after my skin has been thus destroyed, then in my flesh I shall see God, whom I shall see on my side, and my eyes shall behold, and not another." Amen

Sing and/or Listen
"Near to the Heart of God"

https://www.youtube.com/watch?v=2Un-FNHWJ0tA

There is a place of quiet rest,
Near to the heart of God,
A place where sin cannot molest,
Near to the heart of God.
O Jesus, blest Redeemer,
Sent from the heart of God,
Hold us, who wait before Thee,
Near to the heart of God.
- The UM Hymnal Number 472
Pray
Gracious God, there are many distractions and I am pulled in different directions. I try and must respond to multiple and often conflicting needs. Draw me more deeply into your presence and give me strength of endure. Amen.

The Spiritual Discipline of Journaling

1. Read the selected scripture passage. Record your immediate thoughts.

2. Read the devotion/reflection for today. Record your thoughts and/or write your personal reflections.

3. Prayerfully listen for God's message to you. Record what you hear from the Lord.

4. Pray the prayer that is written and/or record and pray your own prayer.

5. Conclude with praise and worship. Use the suggested hymn from YouTube or choose another.

THE FOURTH SUNDAY OF EASTER
John 10:22-30

"I am the good shepherd. I know my own and my own know me, just as the Father knows me and I know the Father. And I lay down my life for the sheep. I have other sheep that do not belong to this fold. I must bring them also, and they will listen to my voice. So there will be one flock, one shepherd. For this reason the Father loves me, because I lay down my life in order to take it up again. No one takes it from me, but I lay it down of my own accord. I have power to lay it down, and I have power to take it up again. I have received this command from my Father . . . . My sheep hear my voice. I know them, and they follow me. I give them eternal life, and they will never perish. No one will snatch them out of my hand. What my Father has given me is greater than all else, and no one can snatch it out of the Father's hand. The Father and I are one."

"Two Images for a High-Tech World"

Who does Jesus say he is? A CEO? A Career Coach? Mentor? Quarterback? Example? Hero? No! No! None of that. Rather, in his own words, Jesus says, "I am the Good Shepherd."

Who does Jesus say you are? He says, "My sheep." This means you are: a treasured person rather than a pawn; a precious son/daughter rather than a savage; someone who counts rather than someone just to be counted! Yes, of course!

In the lectionary gospel for today, what does Jesus say he has done for you? In his own words, "the good shepherd lays down his life for his sheep." No question in the gospel about his personal sacrifice. We know the story! They crucified him. By three o'clock on Good Friday afternoon he was stone-cold-dead and by sundown his body was placed in the tomb. His end was agonizing, violent, bloody, dark, and destructive.

These two images - the Good Shepherd and his sheep - are very close together in the gospel lesson for the fourth Sunday of Easter. Moreover, they are very close together in us and impact our lives profoundly in this high-tech world.

All that remains is for you to believe this incredible truth about yourself, that you are his sheep. That means nobility stirs within you, that you are special, that you are son/daughter of awesome God, that you belong to the Good Shepherd.

The conviction that we are his sheep compels us to do what's Christian in a high-tech world, for the whisper of dignity in your soul will not let you do less.

Sing and/or Listen!

https://www.youtube.com/watch?v=aC9r_oNK yf8

Take my life, and let it be
consecrated, Lord, to thee.
Take my moments and my days,
let them flow in ceaseless praise.

Take my hands, and let them move
at the impulse of thy love.
Take my feet, and let them be,
swift and beautiful for thee.
The United Methodist Hymnal, No. 399

Pray

Good Shepherd, help me to do what you command in the places where I live and work. Amen

The Spiritual Discipline of Journaling

1. Read the selected scripture passage.
Record your immediate thoughts.

2. Read the devotion/reflection for today.
Record your thoughts and/or write your personal reflections.

3. Prayerfully listen for God's message to you.
Record what you hear from the Lord.

4. Pray the prayer that is written and/or record
and pray your own prayer.

5. Conclude with praise and worship. Use the
suggested hymn from YouTube or choose another.

Monday

"Trust the Good Shepherd!"

Read John 10: 27-28

"My sheep hear my voice. I know them, and they follow me. I give them eternal life."

"The Gift of Eternal Life"

Now, let us move beyond the call to follow the Good Shepherd to his incredible promise. Not only does he say "My sheep hear my voice . . . and they follow me," but he also says, "I give them eternal life." That's wonderful news in this high-tech world. No one else but Jesus can do that for us.

The truth is that scientists and doctors cannot do it. High-tech science and medicine are unable to resolve the most destructive fact of existence. Despite sassy commercials, classy sound bites, flashy media productions, and upscale health treatment, death is still the end of the line. However advanced this age in which we live, no one escapes the grim reaper, not even good people like you.

My guess is that some remember Katie Couric from the Today Show on NBC. She was the co-anchor of this highly successful news program. When her husband Jay Monahan was diagnosed with colon cancer, she put passionate energy into trying to save him. She did not sit around "being sad." She went on the offensive and funneled her enormous energy and research skills into finding help for husband Jay. She used 20 years of research and reporting experience to find out everything she could about the disease. Despite her efforts and the very best of high-tech medicine, he died of cancer in early 1998, leaving Katie Couric a single mother of two young daughters.

It matters not that one lives in a high tech-age like this with high tech medicine and science. Life still ends with death. Nothing has changed in that respect. It is a battle to the finish. No compromise. No technical knockouts. The grim reaper finally takes all.

In the face of that ultimate despair, the Good Shepherd makes a radical and incredible promise. His last word is not about death but life. "My sheep hear my voice. I know them, and they follow me. I give them eternal life."

The good news is that the Good Shepherd has given you the gift of eternal life. Rejoice and be glad!

'Tis so sweet to trust in Jesus,
and to take him at his word;
just to rest upon his promise,
and to know, "Thus saith the Lord."

Jesus, Jesus, how I trust him!
How I've proved him o'er and o'er!
Jesus, Jesus, precious Jesus!
O for grace to trust him more!

- The United Methodist Hymnal Number 462

Listen and/or Sing

https://www.youtube.com/watch?v=3RqfAjPzpko

Pray

Lord Jesus, I love you because you first loved me. I trust you for my life and salvation. Keep this faith alive in me. Amen.

The Spiritual Discipline of Journaling

1. Read the selected scripture passage. Record your immediate thoughts.

2. Read the devotion/reflection for today. Record your thoughts and/or write your personal reflections.

3. Prayerfully listen for God's message to you. Record what you hear from the Lord.

4. Pray the prayer that is written and/or record and pray your own prayer.

5. Conclude with praise and worship. Use the suggested hymn from YouTube or choose another.

"The Family of Christ!"

1 Peter 2:2-10
"Come to him, a living stone, though rejected
by mortals yet chosen and precious in God's
sight, and like living stones, let yourselves be
built into a spiritual house, to be a holy priesthood, to offer spiritual sacrifices acceptable to
God through Jesus Christ . . .. you are a chosen
race, a royal priesthood, a holy nation, God's
own people, in order that you may proclaim the
mighty acts of him who called you out of darkness into his marvelous light. Once you were
not a people, but now you are God's people;
once you had not received mercy, but now you
have received mercy."

"Let the local church family be the Church
Triumphant!"
The family of Christ is made up of sophisti-
cated and busy people. We make movies, fly in

airplanes, and build microscopes. We work, invent, play, mingle, and become inspired; we love, have families and friends.

The family of Christ is also made up of poor people who are hungry and thirsty, sick and in prison, homeless and displaced. They are sometimes featured on television, in newspapers, and on the Internet. We have old people dying in their wheelchairs; infants screaming from hunger and/or dirty diapers; people despairing because their homes were destroyed.

The family of Christ include millions of people whose lives have been high jacked by poverty, sickness, illiteracy, alcohol, nicotine, and materialism, as well as young and old who have been abandoned. No one, absolutely no one, is disqualified from God's love. Everyone matters to Jesus.

The family of Christ is not limited to clean, well-dressed, church-attending, lawn-mowing, home owning, Tax-paying College graduates. His family circle is also inclusive of a raggedy assortment of poor people, homeless people, illiterate people, drug addicted people, high school drop-outs, illegal aliens - and most of them aren't dressed right, don't speak right, don't act right, don't live the way we do - just the sort of people you wouldn't dream of inviting to your house.

Nevertheless, think of the family of Christ as "a chosen race, a royal priesthood, a holy nation, God's own people." Amazing! How can this be? It is the work of Jesus through the Holy Spirit.

Here's the good news.

• You don't have to have a college degree to be in the family of Christ.

• You don't have to be an ordained minister or priest to be in the family of Christ.

• You don't have to make your subjects and your verbs agree to be in the family of Christ.

• You don't have to be a Republican or a Democrat to be in the family of Christ.

• You don't have to be young or old to be in the family of Christ.

• You only need a heart full of grace and goodwill.

114

• A heart that cares like Jesus is a heart that pleases God.

"You are a chosen race, a royal priesthood, a holy nation, God's own people, in order that you may proclaim the mighty acts of him who called you out of darkness into his marvelous light."

Sing and/or Listen
https://www.youtube.com/watch?v=WtCV_ysZ
CO4
Let the anthems ring out, songs of victory swell
For the church triumphant, is alive and well. -
Bill Gaither

Pray

Yes, Lord, I rejoice that you have accepted me in the church triumphant. Help me to celebrate the face of it for as long as I live on planet earth. Amen.

The Spiritual Discipline of Journaling

1. Read the selected scripture passage.

2. Read the devotion/reflection for today. Record your thoughts and/or write your personal reflections.

3. Prayerfully listen for God's message to you. Record what you hear from the Lord.

4. Pray the prayer that is written and/or record and pray your own prayer.

5. Conclude with praise and worship. Use the suggested hymn from YouTube or choose another.

Wednesday

"A prayer for the end of life!"

Acts 7:54-60

"When they heard these things, they became enraged and ground their teeth at Stephen. But filled with the Holy Spirit, he gazed into heaven and saw the glory of God and Jesus standing at the right hand of God. 'Look,' he said, 'I see the heavens opened and the Son of Man standing at the right hand of God!' But they covered their ears, and with a loud shout all rushed together against him. Then they dragged him out of the city and began to stone him; and the witnesses laid their coats at the feet of a young man named Saul. While they were stoning Stephen, he prayed, 'Lord Jesus, receive my spirit.' Then he knelt down and cried out in a loud voice, 'Lord, do not hold this sin against them.' When he had said this, he died."

"Lord Jesus, receive my spirit."

Stephen was a committed Christian. Nevertheless, "They dragged him out of the city and

117

began to stone him" and they stoned him to death. He was not afraid.

Lieutenant William G. Farrow was executed by the enemy during the Second World War. One of his letters was found in the files of the War Ministry Building, along with the last messages of those condemned with him. The letters were used as evidence in the war crimes trials of persons accused of executing the Doolittle fliers, and they were widely publicized at the time. One brief excerpt from Farrow's letter appeared in newspapers all over the country and stirred the hearts of millions of readers.

As the young Lieutenant sat in his cell writing what was to be his last letter, he wasn't thinking of himself, or of the cruel death that awaited him and the two other Doolittle fliers condemned with him. He was thinking of his mother and fiancée. How could he comfort them, except to remind them of the faith that was his own great comfort as he faced death? The time was getting short. He reread what he had written to his mother, and, anxious to spare her as much grief

118

as possible, added these closing words: ". . . My faith in God is complete, so I am unafraid."

Sounds like Stephen in the scripture passage. He prayed, "receive my spirit." "Then he knelt down and cried out in a loud voice 'Lord, do not hold this sin against them.' When he had said this, he died."

"Lord Jesus, receive my spirit." Amen!

Sing and/or Listen!

https://www.youtube.com/watch?v=S8zuyjdQ7
VI
"Precious Lord, take my hand
Lead me on, let me stand
I am tired, I am weak, I am worn
Through the storm, through the night
Lead me on to the light
Take my hand, precious Lord
Lead me home."

Pray

Take my hand precious Lord and lead me on."
Amen

The Spiritual Discipline of Journaling

1. Read the selected scripture passage.
Record your immediate thoughts.

2. Read the devotion/reflection for today.
Record your thoughts and/or write your personal reflections.

3. Prayerfully listen for God's message to you.
Record what you hear from the Lord.

4. Pray the prayer that is written and/or record and pray your own prayer.

5. Conclude with praise and worship. Use the suggested hymn from YouTube or choose another.

Thursday

"Who do you trust for your life?"

John 14:1

"Do not let your hearts be troubled. Believe in God, believe also in me."

"Believe"

"Do not let your hearts be troubled. Believe in God, believe also in me."

Is the Lord instructing us to ignore the thing that is causing our anxiety and making us afraid? Is he advising us to run away from our fears to some amusement park, or to some feverish activity, or to some wild undertaking? None of that! Rather, instead of worrying, Jesus invites his disciples (including us) to trust God and himself.

- If cancer invades your body, "Believe in God, believe also in me."

- If a heart attack sends you to the canvas, "Believe in God, believe also in me."
- If addiction takes you down, "Believe in God, believe also in me."
- If you are shut out, locked out, kept out, pushed out, punched out, left out, "Believe in God, believe also in me."
- If your company is down-sizing, side-sizing, up-sizing, "Believe in God, believe also in me."
- If you are running on empty, "Believe in God, believe also in me."

Who do you trust? Who do I trust? I choose to believe in God and Jesus. I don't know what tomorrow holds but I know who holds tomorrow. This is my Father's world! Amen.

Sing and/or Listen!

https://www.youtube.com/watch?v=Q1hhqr-goZag

"This is my Father's world,
and to my listening ears
all nature sings, and round me rings
the music of the spheres.
This is my Father's world:
I rest me in the thought
of rocks and trees, of skies and seas;
his hand the wonders wrought. "
– The United Methodist Hymnal
Number 144

Pray

King Jesus, I choose this day to believe in God
and believe in you. Reinforce this faith within
me. Amen.

The Spiritual Discipline of Journaling

1. Read the selected scripture passage.
Record your immediate thoughts.

2. Read the devotion/reflection for today.
Record your thoughts and/or write your personal reflections.

3. Prayerfully listen for God's message to you.
Record what you hear from the Lord.

4. Pray the prayer that is written and/or record
and pray your own prayer.

5. Conclude with praise and worship. Use the
suggested hymn from YouTube or choose another.

Friday

"The promise of Christ is good news!"

John 14:1-3

"Do not let your hearts be troubled. Believe in God, believe also in me. [2]In my Father's house there are many dwelling places. If it were not so, would I have told you that I go to prepare a place for you? [3]And if I go and prepare a place for you, I will come again and will take you to myself, so that where I am, there you may be also.

"Living with dying through Jesus Christ!"

We live in the valley of the shadow of death! No one escapes the fact of it. There's no ultimate protection in being young. We are vulnerable. Each day brings us face to face with the fact of it!

125

No one is one hundred percent safe on I-4, or immune to some deadly virus, or insulated against lightening, or bullet proof.

William H. Willimon is a retired bishop of the church. Before that, he was Dean of the Chapel and Professor of Christian Ministry at Duke University. In the forward to his book, **Living with Dying**, he acknowledged his own mortality. "George Lea is dying," he wrote. Then he added, "Of course, so am I. We're both terminal. The difference between George Lea Harper and me is that he knows he's dying whereas I don't. He has stood on the cliff, stooped over, and peered into the dark abyss. He has heard the owl call his name." (Living With Dying, VII)

The truth is that we are all terminal; death is really just a matter of time. Many are in a state of denial about this; nevertheless, we are all living with dying.

Must we despair in the face of that reality? Nope! Rather, we choose to focus on and believe the good news of Jesus' promise. "I have told you that I go to prepare a place for you," he said. "And if I go and prepare a place for you, I will come again and will take you to myself, so that where I am, there you may be also."

Sing and or L sten!
https://www.youtube.com/watch?v=spa7WkwjwGw

Because He lives, I can face tomorrow,
Because He lives, all fear is gone;
Because I know He holds the future,
And life is worth the living,
Just because He lives!
And then one day, I'll cross the river,
I'll fight life's final war with pain;
And then, as death gives way to victory,
I'll see the lights of glory and I'll know He
lives! - The United Methodist Hymnal

Pray

Dear King Jesus! Thank you for preparing a place for me/us in the Father's House. I am comforted by your promise to return and take me/us home. Amen.

The Spiritual Discipline of Journaling

1. Read the selected scripture passage. Record your immediate thoughts.

2. Read the devotion/reflection for today. Record your thoughts and/or write your personal reflections.

3. Prayerfully listen for God's message to you. Record what you hear from the Lord.

4. Pray the prayer that is written and/or record and pray your own prayer.

5. Conclude with praise and worship. Use the suggested hymn from YouTube or choose another.

Saturday

John 14:1-3

Jesus: "I go to prepare a place for you"

"The Place"

Focus on Jesus' promise, "I go to prepare a place for you . . ." Do you believe it? Do I? Does anyone believe Jesus?

Well, yes! I believe that Jesus has gone "to prepare a place." And I'm confident that you, the reader of this devotion, believe this as well.

It's a wonderful feeling to have a place prepared just for you. Isn't it?

When I was a seminary student, Joan and I went to visit my Grandmother "Bam" in Kentucky. Within minutes of our arrival, her daughter who lived next door showed up. Surprise! They had worked for hours just to welcome and be with us. Grandmother "Bam" and Aunt Vivian had done everything imaginable to prepare a place for us. The house was ready, the table was set with her finest silver and China, dinner was prepared, and family was invited. Grandmother was set and waiting for our arrival. She stood at the door and waited, looking for us to drive into her yard. She had prepared a place for us.

That was just terrific and was/is an awesome feeling. The memory is precious to this day, the fifth Sunday of Easter.

At a higher level, Jesus said, "I go to prepare a place for you." I look forward to that place Jesus has prepared, not only for me but for all his disciples. Thank you, Jesus!

Sing and/or Listen!
Swing Low Sweet Chariot
https://www.youtube.com/watch?v=v8frEt6w4G8

Pray
Swing low, sweet chariot coming for to carry me home. Amen.

The Spiritual Discipline of Journaling

1. Read the selected scripture passage.
Record your immediate thoughts.

2. Read the devotion/reflection for today.
Record your thoughts and/or write your personal reflections.

3. Prayerfully listen for God's message to you.
Record what you hear from the Lord.

4. Pray the prayer that is written and/or record and pray your own prayer.

5. Conclude with praise and worship. Use the suggested hymn from YouTube or choose another.

131

THE FIFTH SUNDAY OF EASTER

"The Way Home!"

John 14:1-11

"I go to prepare a place for you ⁴And you know the way to the place where I am going." ⁵Thomas said to him, "Lord, we do not know where you are going. How can we know the way?" Jesus said to him, "I am the way, and the truth, and the life. No one comes to the Father except through me.

"Jesus is the Way!"

There is a quality about "doubting Thomas" that most people admire. Thomas asked the question. Thomas had the courage to express his reservations and uncertainty, while the others simply pretended to understand Jesus, whom they had so often misunderstood.

When Jesus said, "You know the way to the place where I am going," Thomas stopped him: "Lord, we do not know where you are going." Jesus answered by offering the pivotal statement concerning his identity: I am the way, and the truth, and the life. No one comes to the Father except through me"

This is good news. If you have ever had the experience of being lost and have asked directions, only to be given landmarks you couldn't locate and street names that seemed not to exist, you recognized that simply being told to travel in a particular direction would not suffice. To be told to go north, south, east, or west was not enough. But Jesus was/is clear.

Lord, how can we know the way? Jesus didn't tell Thomas to go to Jerusalem or to Bethlehem or to Jericho, and you'll know the way. He wasn't talking about a particular direction in which to travel. *The* way is not simply a road or a town. It is not a geographical point. Neither is *the* way simply a style *of* life. Rather, Jesus offers himself as the way to God.

133

Jesus Christ is the way, the truth, and the life. He is the way home. Amen.

Sing and/or Listen!
Sing the wondrous love of Jesus,
Sing His mercy and His grace.
In the mansions bright and blessed
He'll prepare for us a place.
When we all get to Heaven,
What a day of rejoicing that will be!
When we all see Jesus,
We'll sing and shout the victory!
– The United Methodist Hymnal page 701

https://www.youtube.com/watch?v=6Clws ynwVrl

Pray

King Jesus, I affirm and celebrate that you are the way. Neither life nor death nor anything else in all creation can separate us from your love. I look forward to heaven. Amen.

The Spiritual Discipline of Journaling

1. Read the selected scripture passage.
Record your immediate thoughts.

2. Read the devotion/reflection for today.
Record your thoughts and/or write your personal reflections.

3. Prayerfully listen for God's message to you.
Record what you hear from the Lord.

4. Pray the prayer that is written and/or record
and pray your own prayer.

5. Conclude with praise and worship. Use the
suggested hymn from YouTube or choose another.

Monday

"Christt The King's Promise!"

John 14:1-11
"Do not let your hearts be troubled. Believe in God, believe also in me. In my Father's house there are many dwelling places. If it were not so, would I have told you that I go to prepare a place for you? And if I go and prepare a place for you, I will come again and will take you to myself, so that where I am, there you may be also."

"King Jesus will come again!"

Jessica Stern was a former chemical and biological weapons specialist with the National Security Council. Her job inspired the Hollywood movie, "Peacemaker." As early as 1998 she warned about terrorists. She said that these kinds of groups might turn to extreme violence and weapons of mass destruction because they believe Armageddon is coming and they want to hasten the appearance of the Messiah

The reality is that no one can rush God. Our Heavenly Father has his own time-table and it's not up for vote. My job, your job, is to be ready when Christ comes. Those who are ready will be incredibly blessed.

The good news is that one doesn't have to worry about the future. That's in God's hand. There's a great day coming for all who are prepared for Christ's return.

Think about it like this. Christ the King is the Great Physician, the Prince of Peace, the Lamb of God, the Bread of Life, the Good Shepherd, Living Water, the Savior, the Son of God.

We can live this day and every day to the fullest, assured Christ will arrive on God's schedule and keep his promise. "I will take you to myself," he has assured, "so that where I am, there you may be also." Amen!

Sing and/or Listen!
https://www.youtube.com/watch?v=sDpBy
zZqeQ4

In the bulb there is a flower; in the seed,
an apple tree;
In cocoons, a hidden promise: butterflies will
soon be free!
In the cold and snow of winter there's a spring
that waits to be,
Unrevealed until its season, something God
alone can see.

- The United Methodist Hymnal Number 707

Pray

O God, in Christ's resurrection, we see the future. Help me to be assured of the King's returns. Even though I do not know the timeline, help me to trust that he will keep his word. Amen.

The Spiritual Discipline of Journaling

1. Read the selected scripture passage.
Record your immediate thoughts.

2. Read the devotion/reflection for today.
Record your thoughts and/or write your personal reflections.

3. Prayerfully listen for God's message to you.
Record what you hear from the Lord.

4. Pray the prayer that is written and/or record
and pray your own prayer.

5. Conclude with praise and worship. Use the
suggested hymn from YouTube or choose another.

Tuesday

"God is love."
I John 4:16b

Choose to focus on the love of God!

God is love. In view of this, the question is how to respond to disappointments, frustrations, job loss, poor health, and pastoral transition.

God is love. It is not just what happens to us that matters but what we do with what happens. Life is like a deck of cards. We can't control which hand is dealt to us but we can control the way we play the hand.

God is love. The new reality is that we are in the midst of a pastoral transition. The question is how we will play this hand. However we choose, the good news is that "neither life nor death . . . nor anything else in all creation (not even a pastoral transition) will be able to separate us from the love of God in Christ Jesus our Lord." (4 8:28, 29)

God is love. That was true before your illness or other misfortune. God is love was true all day yesterday, and will be true all day today, and will be true all day tomorrow, and will be true every day until time disappears.

God is love. That is the engine which drives us and fills us with hope, now and evermore.

Sing and/or Listen
"The Love of God"

https://www.youtube.com/watch?v=IeBSv4dQ6
BU

Pray

Loving God, as I continue the journey to Pentecost, I celebrate your unconditional love. Keep me connected to your great love, so that I cannot help but share it with the world. Amen

The Spiritual Discipline of Journaling

1. Read the selected scripture passage. Record your immediate thoughts.

2. Read the devotion/reflection for today. Record your thoughts and/or write your personal reflections.

3. Prayerfully listen for God's message to you. Record what you hear from the Lord.

4. Pray the prayer that is written and/or record and pray your own prayer.

5. Conclude with praise and worship. Use the suggested hymn from YouTube or choose another.

Wednesday

John 14:15-21

"If you love me, you will keep my commandments. . .. They who have my commandments
and keep them are those who love me; and those
who love me will be loved by my Father, and I
will love them and reveal myself to them."

"Do you love Jesus? "

"This is my commandment, that you love one
another as I have loved you." John 15:12

"Loving Jesus"

Do you love Jesus? Do I? Jesus is clear. "If you
love me," he declares, "you will keep my commandments.

Focus on that statement. Occasionally,
church families pass through stormy times.
There are periods of upset and even turmoil. The
sounds and smells of uproar in the church family

are inescapable. The long arm of depression, anger, fear, and misunderstanding spreads throughout.

In view of that reality it is not surprising that Jesus gives us a task and puts us to work. "If you love me," he says to us, "you will keep my commandments."

Let's choose to do it in our church family. This does not mean that we have to agree with each other in matters of politics or economics or health care. Sometimes we do not. Nevertheless,

- We can respect one another.
- We can be civil.
- We can be courteous.
- We can be forgiving.
- We can be supportive.

Let us decide to keep Christ's commandment to "love one another." Storms within the church family will come and go as they have in the past. We will not face them alone. Jesus Christ, the Lord of life, has come alongside us through the Holy Spirit to show us the way. He has promised to guide us home. Moreover, he is now here with the gift of his love.

144

Sing and/or Listen

https://www.youtube.com/watch?v=Beq50vHt8uc

"My Jesus, I love Thee, I know Thou art mine;
For Thee all the follies of sin I resign.
My gracious Redeemer, my Savior art Thou;
If ever I loved Thee, my Jesus, 'tis now.

"I love Thee because Thou has first loved me,
And purchased my pardon on Calvary's tree.
I love Thee for wearing the thorns on Thy brow;
If ever I loved Thee, my Jesus, 'tis now."
-The United Methodist Hymnal Number 172

Pray

My Jesus I love you. For this reason, I choose to love the members of your church family. Sometime it is hard. Help me to do this willingly and without reservation. Forgive me when I fail. Amen.

The Spiritual Discipline of Journaling

1. Read the selected scripture passage. Record your immediate thoughts.

2. Read the devotion/reflection for today. Record your thoughts and/or write your personal reflections.

3. Prayerfully listen for God's message to you. Record what you hear from the Lord.

4. Pray the prayer that is written and/or record and pray your own prayer.

5. Conclude with praise and worship. Use the suggested hymn from YouTube or choose another.

THE SIXTH SUNDAY OF EASTER

"Jesus prayed for us!"

John 17:1-11

"After Jesus had spoken these words, he looked up to heaven and said, 'Father, the hour has come; glorify your Son so that the Son may glorify you, since you have given him authority over all people, to give eternal life to all whom you have given him. And this is eternal life, that they may know you, the only true God, and Jesus Christ whom you have sent. . .. I am asking on their behalf; I am not asking on behalf of the world, but on behalf of those whom you gave me, because they are yours. All mine are yours, and yours are mine; and I have been glorified in them. And now I am no longer in the world, but they are in the world, and I am coming to you. Holy Father, protect them in your name that you have given me, so that they may be one, as we are one.'"

"Jesus' prayer for us"

Is it surprising that Jesus prayed "Father" in his prayer for the disciples at the Last Supper? There was something extraordinary about the Divine Father/Son relationship. It was genuine intimacy – tenderness, caring, trusting, closeness, understanding, respect, affection, and love.

In view of that special relationship to his Heavenly Father, Jesus wrapped the Apostles in this blanket of prayer. He prayed "I am asking on their behalf; I am not asking on behalf of the world, but on behalf of those whom you gave me, because they are yours. All mine are yours, and yours are mine; and I have been glorified in them."

Just imagine how the disciples must have felt when they heard these prayer words from the lips of Jesus. Here's the question: do we realize the Lord also included us in the prayer? Yes, he did! He prayed: "I ask not only on behalf of these, but also on behalf of those who will believe in me through their word."

It is clear that Jesus included us in this great prayer. Therefore, we move forward in the confidence that we are forever covered by the prayer of Christ the King. Praise God!

Sing and or Listen!
https://www.youtube.com/watch?v=oYCv4rv7
Duo

Praise God from Whom all blessings flow,
Praise Him all creatures here below,
Praise Him above, ye heavenly host,
Praise Father, Son, and Holy Ghost.
- The United Methodist Hymnal Number 95

The Spiritual Discipline of Journaling

1. Read the selected scripture passage.
Record your immediate thoughts.

2. Read the devotion/reflection for today.
Record your thoughts and/or write your personal reflections.

3. Prayerfully listen for God's message to you.
Record what you hear from the Lord.

4. Pray the prayer that is written and/or record
and pray your own prayer.

5. Conclude with praise and worship. Use the
suggested hymn from YouTube or choose another.

Made in the USA
Columbia, SC
23 March 2018